# IT'S NOT ABOUT THE MONEY

## unmasking mammon

by Jan Kupecz & Ray Borg

Published by Compass Europe

## CONTENTS

It's Not About The Money: unmasking mammon

Copyright: Jan Kupecz and Ray Borg

Published by Compass - finances God's way - Europe

ISBN: 978-90-830317-4-3

contact@compass1.eu
www.compass1.eu

You will note that right from the beginning we state that this book is not about money—and yet, you will see the word money throughout the book.

We ask that you keep an open mind and heart and ask God to prepare your spirit to receive the message of this book. We invite you to use Ephesians 1:17-20 as a prayer before you begin.

"Father, give me the Spirit of wisdom and revelation so that I may know You better. I pray that as I read this book, the eyes of my heart may be enlightened in order that I may know the hope to which you have called me, the riches of Your glorious inheritance in Your holy people and Your incomparably great power for us who believe."

As you begin, take a few moments and ask yourself these questions:

1.  Is my relationship with money affecting my relationship with Jesus?

2.  Who and what influences my spending decisions?

3.  What does the Bible mean when it says we cannot serve both God and mammon?

# Dear Pastor

Your role as pastor has undergone many changes in the last century, but one thing has remained unchanged.

Jesus said, "Go make disciples of all nations, baptizing them in the name of the Father and of the Son and of the Holy Spirit, and teaching them to obey everything I have commanded you."

The disciples in Jesus' day, upon hearing that commission, could not have envisioned the current, complex western society in which we live.

It has a unique set of challenges, deceptions and anxieties.
In the midst of this, one thing is certain; Jesus is still calling His Church to bring the message of truth, grace, salvation and transformation to the human soul.

It is our prayer, that as a pastor, you will read this small book and consider whether financial discipleship needs to have a higher priority in the life of your people and perhaps your own.

We also pray you will recognize that while discipleship is appreciated by most believers, financial discipleship is not.

*Every day, we choose to live with an earthly view of life or to live with eternity in view.*

# Chapter 1

## Discipleship

This book is not about money. It is a book about discipleship.

There are two main themes in the Bible, redemption and stewardship.
Redemption is God reaching out to save us and stewardship is our response.

We must choose to live our lives in thankfulness and acknowledgement of His grace and mercy. For the Christian, we want to live and grow as a disciple of Jesus Christ, the One who redeemed us.
The dictionary definition of a disciple is: follower, someone who adheres to the teaching of another, a learner. A disciple of Jesus Christ is much more than that.

We have been

- united to Jesus by faith (Romans 6:5),
- made alive in him by grace (Ephesians 2:4-5), and
- counted righteous in him because of his work (Galatians 2:16).

Jesus, in all of his supremacy, is also our shepherd—so we know his voice (John 10:27).

As disciples of Jesus Christ, we seek to do more than follow his teachings, we worship Him, we serve Him and we strive to live in a way that is pleasing to Him and what honours His sacrifice.

Pastor Jonathan Parnell puts it this way.

- Jesus is the one to whom all authority in heaven and earth has been given (Matthew 28:18).
- Jesus is the one of whom it will be said, forever, 'Worthy is the Lamb who was slain, to receive power and wealth and wisdom and might and honor and glory and blessing!' (Revelation 5:12)
- He's the one to whom every knee will bow (Philippians 2:10)
- and the one on account of whom all the tribes of the earth will wail (Revelation 1:7),
- and from whom the fury of God's wrath will be executed

Jesus has that kind of supremacy— so what He says matters."

As you read through this little book, keep in mind that as believers, in all areas of our lives, we are somewhere along the path of becoming more like Jesus—discipleship.

Consider that this path of discipleship looks something like this:

- We recognize sin in our life
- We acknowledge that we need God's help
- We repent and ask for help to overcome
- We surrender to the work of the Holy Spirit to daily overcome
- and live righteously
- We hold ourselves accountable to God and others so that we may more fully serve Him and His Kingdom.

The journey of discipleship is life-long and begins with the moment we recognize our need for God's grace and redemption.

As we grow and surrender to Jesus, the Holy Spirit continues to convict us of areas in our lives that need alignment with God's Holy Word—and so the cycle is never ending, until that day we stand before God longing to hear those wonderful words;

*"Well done, good and faithful servant! You have been
faithful with a few things; I will put you in charge of many
things. Come and share your master's happiness!"*
*Matthew 25:23*

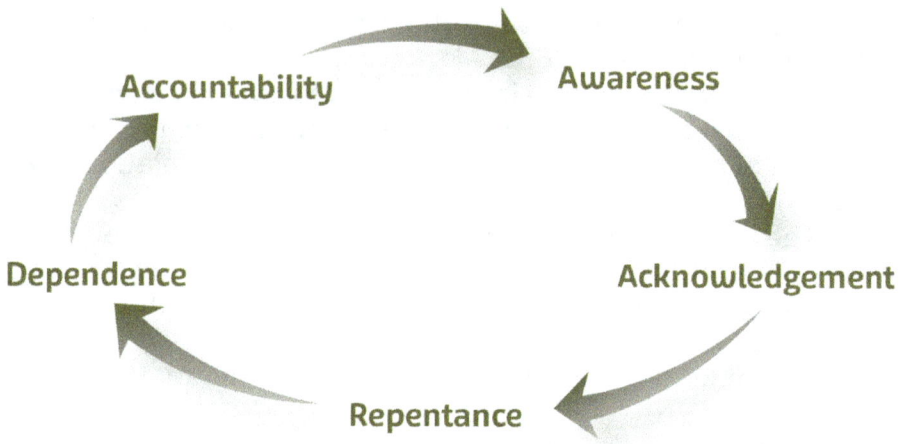

We are dependent upon the ongoing work of the Holy Spirit.

We understand that transformation to becoming like Christ is
only possible in the power of the Holy Spirit when we ask.

It is our hope that somewhere in the reading of this little book,
you will have an "aha" moment within the context of the role of
money in your life and your discipleship journey, a revelation from
God that will perhaps lead you into a deeper relationship with
Him.

"We can know the right words yet never be changed.
This is the difference between information and transformation."
—A.W. Tozer

# Chapter 2

## Living Counter- culturally

With money we buy and sell—it is the economic system of this world. We use money as currency. We work at jobs to earn money to purchase food, clothing, shelter and "things".

- We pay our taxes;
- we spend our money on needs and wants;
- we use money to pay our debts;
- we save money for fun things and emergencies;
- we invest money for our future; and
- we give to God and others.

For many of us, this represents not just what we can do with our money, but also the order under which we prioritize it. Notice that, other than the last point, everything is about us. Even paying taxes is about "us", it is the collective "we".
Psalm 24:1 says—

> *"The earth is the Lord's and all it contains."*

We also read in Deut. 10:14

> *"To the Lord your God belong the heavens, even the highest heavens, the earth and everything in it."*

God is the owner. We are His managers, caretakers, agents, curators, guardians, and custodians. The biblical worldview then is that we have a "stewardship" responsibility, not owners' rights.

Today's western culture, promotes "me-first" thinking and many of us have developed a sense of entitlement from life. We believe that we are deserving of a certain lifestyle: money, large homes, vacations, nicer cars, and stuff that brings a sense of immediate fulfillment and accomplishment. The culture around us promotes this as the abundant life.

> *Nowhere does it say that God has transferred ownership of anything to us. He has however, transferred the responsibility to us.*

Jesus spoke about the "abundant life" but it had nothing to do with having lots of stuff. It was about restoring our relationship to what it had once been, an intimate relationship with God, fulfilling the deepest desire of our souls.

Living counter-culturally is a challenge, especially in the area of our finances. The ever-increasing rise in consumer debt, the increased conflict in marriages and families due to financial stress, increase in anxiety and anxiety related illnesses along with the downward trend in giving is evidence of this. Reports indicate that money issues are one of the top two stressors for Canadians. God's economy is different. It is one of giving and receiving, sowing and reaping, not just buying and selling.

Consider these stats:
- An Ipsos survey released in 2017 showed that 52% of Canadians are just $200 away from financial insolvency at the end of each month. Nearly 1/3 said they do not make enough to cover their expenses.

- At the end of 2017, Statistics Canada reported that debt to income ratio increased to 171%. This means that for every dollar a household makes, they owe $1.71 (this includes consumer debt, mortgages and non-mortgage loans). This number has been climbing for decades and is at an all time high.

- Households with over $50,000 in total income account for 75% for all debt in Canada with half of that number making over $100,000. That means this is not a "poverty issue"

These stats are speaking about Canadians in general. A Christian Canadian study released in 2010 indicated that 1/3 of people in the pew identified as being on the edge of a financial crisis. God's people are not living much differently than the general population.

> *"I came so they can have real and eternal life,*
> *more and better life than they ever dreamed of."*
> *John 10:10 MSG*

Money is neither good nor bad. Jesus did not identify it as either. Money itself is neutral, so why this warning:

> *"For the love of money is a root of all kinds of evil. Some people, eager for money, have wandered from the faith and pierced themselves with many griefs." 1 Timothy 6:10*

This often—misquoted verse is a tough one for most believers. We see this in the lives of others, but rarely in our own lives.

However, if we are truly honest with ourselves, we have to say that we love having money and further, we do not really want to change our spending habits. Here's the thing though—it is not about the money! It is about following Jesus.

In his book, Dethroning Mammon (Lent reflections of 2017) the

Archbishop of Canterbury, Justin Welby, says this:

"Christians should see more clearly, because we have seen Jesus. We are people whose vision has been challenged and corrected, so that we can see the world as it properly is. But seeing badly is still a big problem for most of us most of the time; when we see God and the world wrongly, the problem becomes an issue of great menace. Jesus spent most of his ministry sorting out the mis-seeing of others.
The resurrection was the biggest sight-correction of all."

To participate with God in building His Kingdom on earth, we need to ensure that our influence is from Christ.

When our vision becomes distorted by non-godly influences in our lives, we need a sight-correction.

*"No one can serve two masters; for either he will hate the one and love the other, or else he will be loyal to the one and despise the other. You cannot serve God and mammon." —Matthew 6:24*

# Chapter 3

## The Battle for our Allegiance

Could there be a battle for our allegiance? As Christians, we desire to surrender our lives to the One who gave His so that we can love God completely and utterly.

The choice we face daily is whether we will follow our own desires or God's desires. Even when our heads are clear and our hearts seemingly willing, bringing our behaviours in line with the commands and teachings of Jesus can be a battle.

Could it be that those influences described in Ephesians 6:13, spiritual powers and principalities are vying for our allegiance? Could it be that in this area of money and possessions, the battle is especially fierce?

To understand the battle we face more fully, consider the following words of Jesus. Luke 16:13 (NKJV)

> *"No one can serve two masters, for either he will hate the one and love the other, or else he will be loyal to the one and despise the other. You cannot serve both God and mammon."*

In the above verse, Jesus personifies mammon and even gives it the status of a false god, an idol. He goes further to deliver an all or nothing claim that we cannot worship both. We must choose.

> *Mammon is basically the spirit of the world—and that spirit is a liar.*

These verses suggest there is a conflict or battle between two 'masters'. What exactly does that mean? In dictionaries, the word 'mammon' is generally understood to be "wealth, possessions and may relate to 'that in which one trusts' or in other words 'an evil master that enslaves' or 'any entity that promises wealth'". Another definition is this—"wealth regarded as an evil influence or false object of worship and devotion."

"Mammon" is the Aramaic translation for money. It was also thought to be the name of the ancient Syrian god of riches. Perhaps

Jesus was doing more than just personifying mammon—perhaps as some scholars suggest, Jesus was referring to an entity.

Robert Morris puts it this way;

"Did you know that all money has a spirit on it? It either has the Spirit of God or the spirit of mammon. Money that is submitted to God and His purposes has the Spirit of God on it.
On the other hand, money that is not submitted to God has the spirit of mammon by default. That's why people think money can bring them happiness or fulfillment. Mammon is basically the spirit of the world—and that spirit is a liar."

This spirit of mammon is pervasive and yet subtle, and it can be difficult to detect unless we remain vigilant against it. This spirit tries to persuade us to trust money more than we trust God.

We have a choice: we can choose to either let the spirit of mammon influence what we do with money or allow the Spirit of God to teach us how to manage it. If we fail to make a choice, by default, the spirit of mammon will govern us in this area.
We must be diligent and see which spirit influences us when it comes to the financial realm.

## The spirit of mammon is in direct contrast to the Word of God.

| The Spirit of mammon | The Word of God says ... |
| --- | --- |
| Says "buy and keep" | Remember this: Whoever sows sparingly will also reap sparingly, and whoever sows generously will also reap generously. (2 Cor 9:6) |
| Says "you may not have enough" | And my God will meet all your needs according to the riches of his glory in Christ Jesus. (Phil 4:19) |
| Promotes self- centeredness | Freely you have received; freely give. (Matthew 10:8) |
| Tells us to focus on wants | But seek first his kingdom and his righteousness, and all these things will be given to you as well. (Matthew 6:33) |
| Is selfish | Each of you should give what you have decided in your heart to give, not reluctantly or under compulsion, for God loves a cheerful giver. (2 Cor 9:7) |
| Causes us to feel overwhelmed or intimidated by money, creating fear and anxiety | Do not be anxious about anything, but in every situation, by prayer and petition, with thanksgiving, present your requests to God. And the peace of God, which transcends all understanding, will guard your hearts and your minds in Christ Jesus. (Phil 4:6) |

The spirit of mammon's biggest deception is the promise to give what only God can give:

Identity             Peace
Security             Joy
Significance         Love

Money cannot buy these blessings from God.

The objective of the spirit of mammon is to steal our trust in God. It distorts our vision of God's truth and His blessings.

*Jesus recognized the seduction and the one who was behind it.*

The spirit of mammon tempts us to trust in either riches or ourselves. Jesus himself experienced this temptation.

In Matthew 4: 8-10 when the enemy offered Jesus the kingdoms of the earth and their wealth, Jesus quotes Scripture and responds that He would serve God only. Jesus recognized the seduction and the one who was behind it.

Our world has firmly adopted the principles of "behavioural sciences". The advertising community has studied and analyzed who buys what and why they buy it. As a result, they have learned how to "create needs" within us. They may know more about you and your desires than you do.

The rich, young ruler (Matthew 19:16-22) who meets Jesus face-to- face, chooses instead to trust more in his own riches. The world tells us that money matters almost more than anything else does.

Jesus tells us it is the least important in the Kingdom of God. Trusting in riches makes us its servants and that is why we must choose for ourselves whether to serve God or mammon. The spirit of mammon does not want us or need us to acknowledge its existence —this is perhaps one of its greatest weapons. Most of us live without acknowledging the influence of this spirit.

This does not mean that we have a "get out of jail free" card because "the devil made me do it". On the contrary, the acknowledgement that the enemy of God is at work in this area of our lives should draw us closer to God, to seek His truth and His way.

Everyday, in every way, we must choose to either follow our own desires, (whether influenced by people, our culture or enemies of God), or follow Jesus, our Lord and Redeemer. As we grow deeper in our relationship with Jesus, we should start to see a closer alignment between our plans for our life and God's plan for our life.
Those that live in obedience to God's plan for our money testify to this joy as they surrender more and more to God.
As believers, we may tithe, give offerings and charitable gifts but beyond that, not consider our money to be within the scope of our spiritual journey.

In the church, we discuss some principles of money like, "new testament or old testament", "under the law or under grace", "gross or net", but we fail to dig much deeper in terms of our journey of surrender to Jesus and examine how money impacts that journey.

The spirit of mammon does not satisfy.
It does not offer us the same commitment or contentment as God. By contrast, God promises never to abandon or forsake us, as in Hebrews 13:5.

> *"Keep your lives free from the love of money and be content with what you have, because God has said, 'Never will I leave you;*
> *never will I forsake you.'"*

On the next page are are some symptoms of being under the influence of the spirit of mammon.

1. Worry and anxiety over money
2. Money mismanagement
3. Consistent financial lack
4. "I can't afford it" mentality
5. Impulse buying
6. Stinginess
7. Greed
8. Discontentment
9. Bondage to debt
10. Pride of generosity
11. Exaggerated emphasis on money and an overestimate of its true power

Take some time to re-read this list and consider whether you are experiencing some of these symptoms.
Awareness of what shapes our thinking enables us to ensure that our influence is Christ, not mammon.

For Christians this leads to a sense of shame, guilt and condemnation, which the enemy uses to keep us in turmoil and captivity. God has provided a way through the finished work of the cross. Jesus has set the captives free.

By His death and resurrection, we become free of shame and condemnation, to walk in freedom.
This also applies to the management of our money and possessions —what a wonderful gift.

*Could every spending decision be a spiritual decision?*

# Chapter 4

## A Revelation of the Heart

Martin Luther said that there are three conversions:
the head, the heart and the purse. We give our attention to the
first two parts, but rarely to the pocketbook.

If Martin Luther was correct, then the area of finances matters in
our journey of following Jesus—financial discipleship then is not
about the money, it is about the surrender to Jesus.
Our experiences, beliefs, what we have been taught and observed
in our formative years find residence in the heart. So we need to
ask ourselves—is it reliable? God says the heart is deceitful. Jeremiah 17:9 & 10 put it this way:

> *"The heart is deceitful about all things and beyond cure.*
> *Who can understand it?*
> *I the Lord search the heart and examine the*
> *mind, to reward a man according to his conduct,*
> *according to what his deeds deserve."*

Money often is a temptation, which at its very heart causes us to
rely on it rather than on God as our source of contentment. As
humans, we like or prefer what we can see and touch to what God
promises and gives. This in essence is idolatry.

Many of us have not considered the surrender of our wallets to
the Lord as an act of discipleship, allowing Him to lead and guide
as to its contents and overall purposes.

How we spend, manage and invest our money is a reflection of our spiritual condition and priorities.

The question then is whether we can live lives fully surrendered to God if we do not address the pocketbook.
The book, Wealth, Riches and Money by authors Earl Pitts and Craig Hill says this:

"In church we teach on tithing, giving, sowing and reaping, prosperity, but leave people to their own devices and perhaps vices regarding the management of their own personal consumption. Most people are then highly influenced by the spirit of mammon and never really understand what is happening to them long-term."

Money has a key role on our journey as a disciple of Christ.
As our relationship with Jesus grows and we mature as His disciples, we want to protect our intimacy with Him and keep growing.

We are prepared to let go of our desires and our need to control the direction of our lives and to yield to His greater plan and purposes for our lives. Often this is not an easy or an immediate process but takes time and consistent determination.

*Surrender is not giving up—*
*it is giving in.*

It is important not to allow the spirit of mammon to take us off course from finishing strong and completing our eternal assignment. We need to appreciate the wealth the Lord has provided and allows us to create—but we hurt ourselves if we love it more than we love God. Wealth is a tool through which we can bless others. When we trust God instead of earthly riches, we can give generously in the same spirit He gave His Son to us.

As we learn what the Bible says about financial discipleship, it needs to become more than factual and informational—we need a revelation of the heart. For it is in that place, where real change takes place—affecting our thinking, beliefs and habits.
It is important to remember that God is the Source—our source for all that we need.

Proverbs 3:5-10 also reminds us that He is the Source.

> *"Trust in the Lord with all your heart, and lean not on our own understanding; in all your ways acknowledge Him, and He shall direct your paths.*
> *Do not be wise in your own eyes; fear the Lord and depart from evil.*
> *It will be health to your flesh, and strength to your bones.*
> *Honour the Lord with your possessions and with the first fruits of all your increase; so your barns will be filled with plenty, and your vats will overflow with new wine".*

God is looking to fulfill our needs but it begins by us looking to Him as the Source. We must seek to be intentional in avoiding any seduction of the spirit of mammon and the systems of the world.

# Chapter 5

## The Way Forward

If the Holy Spirit has created some awareness in your heart, the next step is to acknowledge His nudging. The journey of a disciple of Jesus is one marked with repeated awareness, repentance and transformation.
When we allow God to transform areas of our lives, we come truly alive. We feel His pleasure. God calls us to be holy—to be set apart for Him.

God is the source of our supply; He is the one we depend on— not a job, nor the world's economy but on God's provision and God's economy. God is our Source and Provider.

The next step, whether our disobedience was a result of ignorance or wilfulness, is to repent in order to make a way towards a re-stored relationship with the Father and the management of our money and possessions.

You might want to pray something like the following:

"Dear God, forgive me for serving another master. Forgive me for trusting in other sources when you are the Source. Forgive me for my selfishness, pride and covetousness. Forgive my 'fear of lack' ruling my life. Forgive me for not surrendering my money and possessions to your Lordship and leading. Please forgive me for listening to the unholy spirit of mammon.

Lord, I ask you to break that spirit from my family, my descendants, and myself. Wash me clean from any lingering influences or affects from being under this spirit's control. Set me free from any love of money rooted in my heart.

Help me this day to walk according to your Word's directions in the area of financial stewardship, led by your Spirit in how to manage my money and possessions, wisely and generously, being an extravagant giver to the kingdom of God. Amen."

Repentance requires an intentional 'turning away' or doing things differently. We need to ask the Lord for His help in this process.

*We need to ask Him to show us how to make changes in our thinking, beliefs, habits and behaviour. The next step is to begin to understand what His Word says about this area.*

Begin to study God's Word looking for the truth and His guidance. There are resources for consideration in the final section of this booklet. The disciples did not always get it right the first time, not even the second or third. Likewise, we may start and fall, but we need to get back up again and journey onward, learning from our mistakes and growing in wisdom and understanding in this area. It will require trusting the Lord in this process. Trust does not happen overnight, it takes time to grow and mature—so we should allow ourselves time.

It is by knowing truth and knowing God's voice that we defend against the deceptions of those who would seek to steal, kill, and destroy.

It is our prayer that this booklet has been a helpful tool in your financial discipleship journey.

As Paul said in Philippians 3:14
"I press toward the goal for the prize of the upward call of God in Christ Jesus."

If you have prayed the prayer in this chapter or the content has influenced you in some way, we would love your feedback.

Connect with us at info@compass1.eu

Take some time to dig deeper in your own heart and consider these questions.

1.      How is my relationship with money affecting my relationship with Jesus?

2.      How is every spending decision a spiritual decision?

3.      What evidence is there in my life that the spirit of mammon is competing for my attention?

Dear Reader ...

*What might God be calling me to do next?*

_____

_____

_____

_____

_____

_____

_____

# Chapter 6

# Note to Pastors and Church Leaders

## The Role of the Church

If the stats are any indication, God's people are struggling and our communities for which we are responsible are struggling.

The 2010 Christian survey referred to earlier in this book not only indicated that 1/3 of the people in the pews identified as being on the edge of a financial crisis, it also noted that 87% of those surveyed would never go to their church leadership for financial counsel. Therefore, whether it is due to a financial crisis or general counsel regarding money, Christians are not seeking counsel from their church leaders.

If we as His church do not help people with the "why" and the "how" to live financially sound lives as God's stewards, the information will come from the world—leaving God's people under the influence of the spirit of mammon or the culture of the world.

We believe the "why" is clear in Scripture. The topic of money and possessions occurs in Scripture over 2350 times. Sixteen of Jesus' 38 parables are about money and possessions. Jesus must have understood the importance for his disciples.

The "how" is the practical part of helping God's people get out of debt, if necessary, and manage money in keeping with biblical

principles. We believe that behind every solid financial practice is a biblical principle.
If you separate the two parts, the journey is incomplete.

### Life is in Jesus and Him alone.

Lack of financial discipleship within the whole of disciple making can unwittingly create a barrier towards a deeper relationship with Christ where we experience that joy and peace.

We, His church, need to take back the conversation around finances and place it along the path of discipleship.

We need to preach and teach with integrity and authority to bring God's people out of the worldly systems and through prayer and repentance into Godly living—in all areas.

We want to be the Good News. Our lives should evidence transformation (language, conduct, lifestyle, and yes—money management) so that we can share the hope we have within us, to show the love of Jesus and the way to live new lives surrendered to the One who redeemed us.

*God has called us to 'make a voice' in this area of financial discipleship.*
*We value and appreciate the role of the local church and its discipling ministry.*

Please feel free to connect with us to discuss how we can best support you in your role.
You can connect with us at info@compass1.eu

# Chapter 7

# Resources

We are grateful to many experienced and thoughtful writers, theologians, scholars and pastors who have published their understanding of stewardship and/or the spirit of mammon, whether in book form or articles on the internet. We have borrowed liberally from some of these learned Christians and in our pursuit to make this a highly readable book have intentionally left out a great deal of depth in their teachings.

We wish to thank Earl Pitts, whose writing and teaching in the book and DVD, Wealth, Riches and Money was made available to us at the beginning of our journey—responding to God's call to 'make a voice' for financial discipleship.

Many of the lists in this book come from that book.
This, along with other resources for further study are on our website: www.compass1.eu

Compass provides individual and small group study materials in the area of financial management. We offer free facilitator training and many tools to help individuals and churches learn, apply and teach God's financial principles.

# Monkey Business

This book, written buy the founder of Compass in Europe, Peter Briscoe, tells the story of the parable which Jesus told about a steward who was accused of wasting his master's possessions.

Throughout this parable, Jesus is explaining to us how mammon influences our thinking and actions, and how we can use money in a way which overcomes the power of mammon to serve others and advance the Kingdom of God.

This book and other resources can be ordered from our online shop.  www.compass1.eu/shop

## About Compass

Compass - finances God's way is a global, non-denomination-al movement teaching financial discipleship and generosity. The purpose is to serve churches, businesses, ministries, schools and other organisations by providing biblically-based solutions on handling money and possessions. Our vision is to see everyone, everywhere faithfully living by God's financial principles in all areas of their lives.

## Global mission

Compass' mission is to help people everywhere to learn, apply and teach Gods financial and business principles. We are looking for three major outcomes.

1. To know Christ more intimately as we trust and obey Him,
2. To become free from worry, fear, stress and anxiety and then be free to serve and love the Lord and our neighbours.
3. To contribute to fulfilling the Great Commission by giving our money and other resources to fund the work of the Church.

The Compass Global Team is comprised of local leadership on 6 continents – Europe, Asia, South America, North America, Africa and the Indian sub-continent. Our continental offices serve more than 90 nations around the world.

Compass has developed a wide range of resources in a wide variety of formats, and languages, such as DVD based teaching, workshops, small group studies, e-books and online learning. There are teaching resources for all ages, from small children through students to adults; with application to areas of life such as business, church, marriage and family.
These resources can be seen at www.compass1.eu

Compass is active in over 80 nations over the globe and has re-sources in many languages.
Contact our continental offices through  www.compass1.global

## The Authors

Jan Kupecz is the Executive Director of Financial Discipleship Canada and the Canadian National Christian Foundation. Jan uses her business and leadership experience within her local church teaching, training and discipling.
She also volunteers as a debt coach at the Kerith Debt Freedom Centre, a ministry and outreach of her local church. Jan loves seeing people set free from the burden of debt, embracing hope and a future.

Rev. Ray Borg was a social worker and human resources consultant prior to joining Financial Discipleship Canada as Ministry and Church Liaison. He is a pastor, teacher, conference speaker, and a regular guest on the Let's Talk Money radio programme.
He has seen the impact of poverty and financial hardship on generations around the globe and longs to see people walk in the freedom Jesus Christ has made available for them in all areas of their lives, including money and possessions.

Financial Discipleship Canada is a ministry of the Canadian Compass movement.

## The Book

During Jesus' lifetime of ministry, his passion was to teach the people how to understand the heart of His Father concerning every aspect of their lives. Although the people had come to believe, they often carried out their lives in ways that led them into trouble.

Sometimes the problem was their own heart while at other times it was the failure to recognize that there was someone out to destroy them and influence the culture around them.

A. W. Tozer said, "We can know the right words yet never be changed. This is the difference between information and transformation."

As disciples of Jesus Christ, we seek to be more and more transformed into His likeness. As a result, we find ourselves following His teaching, worshipping Him, and seeking to please Him all because of the sacrifice He has made for each one of us.

This book is about discipleship. It is about an area of our lives that has significant influence and the potential to take us off course.